Baby Reptiles

Bobbie Kalman

Crabtree Publishing Company

www.crabtreebooks.com

It's fun to learn about **Baby Animals**

Created by Bobbie Kalman

Dedicated by Katherine Berti
For Peter, Nicole, Jonathan, and Sienna Szymanski,
with warm wishes for plenty happy smiles,
big hugs, much love, and endless laughter.

**Author and
Editor-in-Chief**
Bobbie Kalman

Editor
Kathy Middleton

Proofreader
Crystal Sikkens

Photo research
Bobbie Kalman
Crystal Sikkens

Design
Bobbie Kalman
Katherine Berti
Samantha Crabtree
(logo and front cover)

Production coordinator
Katherine Berti

Illustrations
Barbara Bedell: pages 9, 13, 24 (eggs, gavials,
komodo dragons, and scales)
Katherine Berti: pages 10, 11, 24 (life cycle
and lizards)
Margaret Amy Salter: pages 7, 24 (bodies)

Photographs
© Dreamstime.com: pages 9 (top),
20 (bottom)
© iStockphoto.com: pages 12 (bottom),
14, 16 (top), 17 (bottom), 23 (top right
and bottom left)
© Lewis Scharpf: page 11 (top)
© Shutterstock.com: All other images

Library and Archives Canada Cataloguing in Publication

Kalman, Bobbie, 1947-
Baby reptiles / Bobbie Kalman.

(It's fun to learn about baby animals)
Includes index.
ISBN 978-0-7787-3954-8 (bound).--ISBN 978-0-7787-3973-9 (pbk.)

1. Reptiles--Infancy--Juvenile literature. I. Title. II. Series.

QL644.2.K214 2008   j597.9'139   C2008-907020-8

Library of Congress Cataloging-in-Publication Data

Kalman, Bobbie.
Baby reptiles / Bobbie Kalman.
p. cm. -- (It's fun to learn about baby animals)
Includes index.
ISBN 978-0-7787-3973-9 (pbk. : alk. paper) -- ISBN 978-0-7787-3954-8
(reinforced library binding : alk. paper)
1. Reptiles--Infancy--Juvenile literature. 2. Reptiles--Juvenile literature. I.
Title. II. Series.

QL644.2.K315 2009
597.9'039--dc22
                                    2008046251

Crabtree Publishing Company

www.crabtreebooks.com   1-800-387-7650

Published in Canada
Crabtree Publishing
616 Welland Ave.
St. Catharines, Ontario
L2M 5V6

Published in the United States
Crabtree Publishing
PMB16A
350 Fifth Ave., Suite 3308
New York, NY 10118

Published in the United Kingdom
Crabtree Publishing
White Cross Mills
High Town, Lancaster
LA1 4XS

Published in Australia
Crabtree Publishing
386 Mt. Alexander Rd.
Ascot Vale (Melbourne)
VIC 3032

What is in this book?

alligator

Many reptiles

Reptiles are animals that have skin made of **scales**. Scales protect a reptile's body. All the animals shown here are reptiles. Alligators, crocodiles, gavials, and caimans belong to one group of reptiles.

caiman

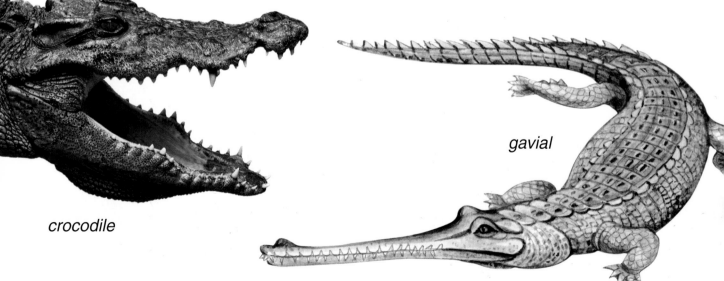

crocodile

gavial

4

snake

Snakes and lizards are other kinds of reptiles.

These lizards are leopard geckos.

Turtles and tortoises are lizards with hard shells on their bodies.
The shells of tortoises are bigger and heavier than the shells of turtles.

turtle

tortoise

Reptile bodies

Reptiles have scales. Snakes have smooth scales. Lizards have rough scales. Turtles and tortoises have shells with hard scales.

hard scales on shell

rough scales on legs

This baby snake has very smooth scales. Its skin feels soft.

This baby bearded dragon is a lizard. It has rough scales all over its body.

Reptiles have **backbones**. Animals with backbones are called **vertebrates**. Vertebrates have **skeletons** made of many bones. Their heads are protected by **skulls**. Some reptiles have four legs. Legs have bones inside them. Sea turtles have flippers instead of legs. Snakes have no legs, but they do have skeletons.

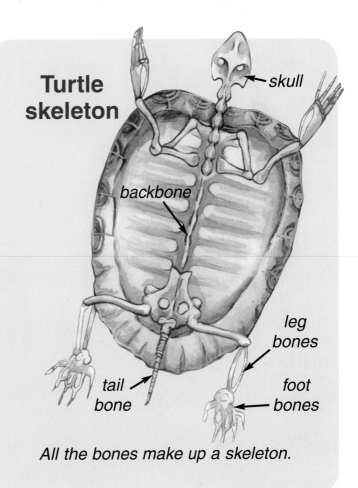

Turtle skeleton

skull

backbone

leg bones

foot bones

tail bone

All the bones make up a skeleton.

baby sea turtle

flipper

Growing new scales

A reptile's scales do not grow with a reptile's body. Reptiles need to **shed**, or lose, their old scales. Shedding scales is called **molting**. Lizards shed their scales in small pieces. They grow new skin under the old skin. This baby lizard is a chameleon.

old scales molting

new scales

This baby gecko is molting. Its body has grown too big for its scales.
Its scales are coming off its head. Soon it will lose all its old skin.

snakeskin

A snake has left its old skin behind. A snake molts its skin in one big piece.

Babies inside eggs

Most reptiles grow inside eggs that their mothers have laid. The babies **hatch**, or break out of the eggs. Baby reptiles look like their parents, but they are smaller. Most mother reptiles do not look after the babies after the babies have hatched.

*Skinks are lizards. This five-lined skink mother has laid a **clutch**, or group of eggs. She guards her eggs for a few weeks, until they hatch. She will then leave the babies alone.*

The eggs of most reptiles have soft shells. This baby skink is hatching from its soft egg.

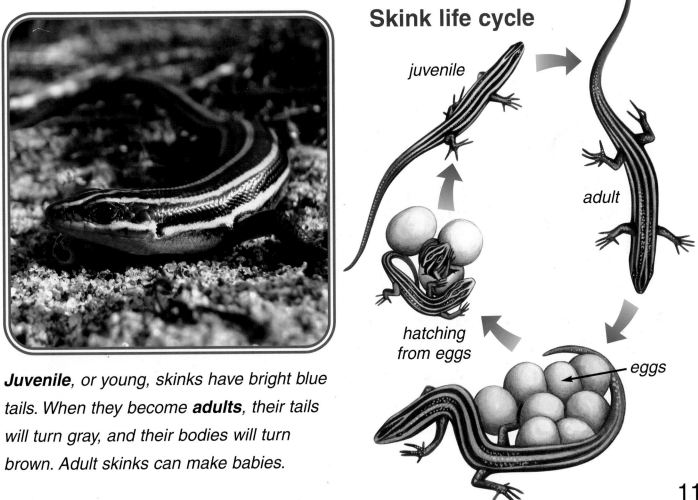

Skink life cycle

juvenile

adult

hatching from eggs

eggs

Juvenile, *or young, skinks have bright blue tails. When they become* **adults**, *their tails will turn gray, and their bodies will turn brown. Adult skinks can make babies.*

Baby lizards

person's finger

Lizards are animals with long bodies and short legs. Some lizards are very small, and some are huge. Most lizards have long tails. When a small lizard is caught by the tail, its tail comes off. A new tail grows back in a few months. Big lizards cannot grow back their tails.

Lizards eat insects. This baby lizard is looking for insects to eat in a flower.

Crested geckos have small hairs on their toes that help them climb.

Chameleons can move each eye in a different direction. They can see two things at once.

This tiny lizard is an anole. It changes its color from green to brown when it is afraid.

Komodo dragons are the largest lizards in the world! Baby Komodo dragons hatch from eggs, as other lizards do.

Baby snakes

Most baby snakes hatch from eggs. The baby green tree pythons shown on these pages hatched from eggs. They look like their parents, but their colors are not the same. The colors change as the snakes grow.

This baby green tree python is hatching from an egg.

Baby pythons are tiny when they hatch. They are thinner than your fingers!

This baby python is bright yellow with red stripes and spots.

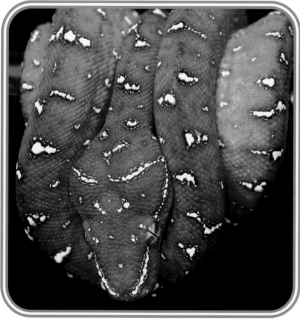

Fully grown green tree pythons are green, yellow, or blue. They live in hot forests. They hunt at night. Pythons wrap themselves around tree branches and hang like this.

This young python is bright orange.

Turtle babies

Sea turtles live in oceans. Mother sea turtles lay eggs as other reptiles do, but first they make a very long trip. They swim back to the same beach where they hatched from eggs.

This leatherback sea turtle swam to the beach where she hatched. She crawls along the sand looking for a safe spot. There, she will dig a hole and lay her eggs in it.

turtle's tail

egg

The mother leatherback is laying her eggs in the hole she dug in the sand.

After 60 days, baby turtles hatch from the eggs. They crawl out of the hole.

baby leatherback turtles

Most of the babies have hatched. They will crawl to the ocean and swim far away.

Gators and crocs

Alligators and crocodiles are huge reptiles, but their babies are small. The alligator above just hatched from an egg. Below, three tiny baby alligators are hanging on to their mother's back.

The mouth of this tiny baby crocodile is tied up. The baby crocodile can bite, even though it is still very small! The caiman below belongs to the crocodile family. It will grow to be huge! All these reptiles live in water.

crocodile

caiman

The gavial is a reptile with a very long, narrow jaw. It has many sharp teeth.

Keeping warm

turtles

Reptiles are **cold-blooded**. Cold-blooded animals cannot make heat inside their bodies. To be healthy, reptiles need to keep warm. One way reptiles warm up is by **basking**, or taking in the sun's heat.

A turtle and a baby alligator are basking. The alligator is warming its belly on the turtle's warm back.

When reptiles are too hot, they go into water. Some reptiles cool off in the shade or under the ground.

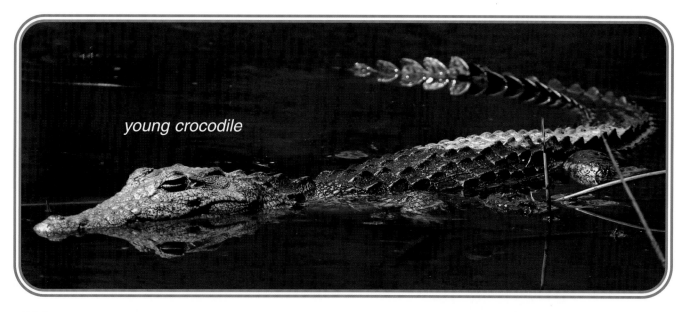

This young crocodile is keeping cool in water, but its back is being warmed by the sun.

These baby geckos are in a cave. They are keeping cool under the cave rock.

More about reptiles

Most reptiles are **carnivores**. They eat other animals. This snake is eating a frog.

There is more to learn about reptiles. What do reptiles eat? How do reptiles breathe? Where do they live? How do they move? These pictures will show you more about reptiles.

iguana

Iguanas are lizards that eat plants. Some turtles also eat mainly plants. There are reptiles that eat both plants and animals.

Reptiles have **lungs** for breathing. Lungs take in air. Some reptiles, such as this sea turtle, live in water. To breathe air, sea turtles must come above water.

leopard
gecko

third eye

Reptiles live in many **habitats**. Habitats are natural places. Most reptiles live in hot **deserts**. Deserts are dry places. Reptiles also live in other habitats, both on land and in water.

These baby reptiles are tuataras. Tuataras belong to their own reptile family. Tuataras have a third eye under the skin of their foreheads.

How do reptiles move?

Reptiles move in different ways.

Alligators and crocodiles can swim and run fast.

Snakes **slither**. They twist and slide.

Many lizards walk and climb. This chameleon is climbing.

Sea turtles swim.

Words to Know and Index

alligators
pages 4, 18, 20, 23

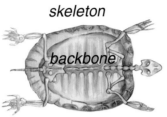
skeleton
backbone

bodies
pages 4, 5, 6–7, 8, 9, 11, 12, 20

crocodiles
pages 4, 18, 19, 21, 23

eggs (hatching)
pages 10, 11, 13, 14, 15, 16, 17, 18

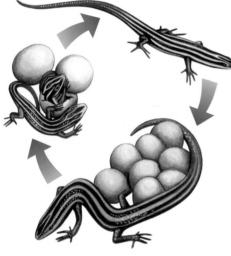

life cycle   pages 10–11

gavials pages 4, 19

lizards
pages 5, 6, 8, 9, 10, 11, 12–13, 21, 22, 23

Komodo dragons
page 13

Other index words

caimans pages 4, 19
cold-blooded page 20
food pages 12, 22
habitats page 23
molting pages 8–9
shells pages 5, 6, 11
tortoises
pages 5, 6

scales
pages 4, 6, 8, 9

snakes
pages 5, 6, 7, 9, 14–15, 23

turtles
pages 5, 6, 7, 16–17, 20, 22, 23

tuataras page 23
vertebrates page 7

Printed in the U.S.A. - BG